THE HIDDEN PATH TO A
Transformed Life

COLIN S. SMITH

Copyright © 2021 by Colin S. Smith
First published in United States in 2020

ISBN: 978-1-7346510-1-0
Design and typeset by Shannon Hannasch
High Note Design, Mason, MI

Published by Unlocking the Bible
PO Box 3454, Barrington, IL 60011
Email: info@unlockingthebible.org
Website: www.unlockingthebible.org

Printed in the United States of America

CONTENTS

Introduction *5*

The Hidden Path

    1. Knowing God................................. 17

    2. Leaving Sin 35

    3. Giving Yourself 57

A Transformed Life

    4. Pursuing the Path 75

    5. Staying the Course......................... 97

    6. Surprised by Joy 115

Endnotes *126*

Acknowledgments.................................. *129*

INTRODUCTION

Why do some people change while others remain essentially the same? And why is it that while some grow in wisdom, others make one foolish choice after another?

Think about people in your life. Some grow and, over time, they enjoy more peace, become more patient, and gain greater self-control. Others seem to carry their sins and failings with them. The same patterns of pride, anger, lust, greed, and laziness that dogged them in the past continue. Change eludes them and, over time, they simply become older versions of what they were before.

No one wants that. So how can we be better? How can you grow in godliness? How can we become more like the Savior we love and trust and follow? That's what I want, and I guess from the fact you have picked up this book that this is what you want too.

Our calling is to move forward, to grow, to mature, and to become better than we were before. Paul challenged Timothy to set an example for other believers "in speech, in conduct, in love, in faith, in purity" (1 Timothy 4:12). He was to pursue these things by devoting himself to reading Scripture and using his God-given gifts. "Practice these things," Paul continued, "so that all may see your *progress*" (4:15, italics added).

Making progress in speech would include learning to soften harsh and hurtful words. Growing in love would involve overcoming coldhearted indifference to the needs of others. Maturing in faith would mean learning to trust God in times of trouble. And making progress in purity would involve a gradual cleansing of hidden impurity in the mind and in the heart.

Progress means growth, becoming more like the Lord Jesus Christ, getting closer to what He calls us to be. So why is it that some who profess faith in Jesus seem to make little progress? The answer, I believe, lies in the title of this book: the path to a transformed life is *hidden*, and some people never find it.

The Bible tells us stories of people who missed the hidden path. Cain, Esau, and Judas are all sad examples. Each of them professed faith: Cain went to worship. Esau was born into a family blessed with the promises of God. Judas was a ministry leader. But none of them found the hidden path to a transformed life.

These stories confront us with the disturbing reality that it is possible to drift through life attending worship, hearing the promises of God, and engaging in ministry without changing, growing, or making progress. When Jesus described the path we are considering, He said, "Those who find it are few" (Matthew 7:14).

The path to a transformed life is hidden. But it can be found. And my prayer is that this book will help you find it.

WHAT IS THE HIDDEN PATH?

Before we begin, we need to name the hidden path. The Bible calls it repentance. Yes, repentance is the hidden path to a transformed life. If that takes you by surprise, it may be that you have picked up a mistaken view of repentance.

Some people think repentance is beating up on yourself for your failures. But if that were true, why would Jesus say there is joy in heaven over a sinner who repents (Luke 15:7)? Why would heaven rejoice over people beating up on themselves?

The words of Jesus make it abundantly clear that repentance is not a miserable journey of self-loathing and regret. Repentance brings joy in heaven, and if there is joy in heaven over repentance, there will be joy in repentance for you.

There's a long-standing joke in our family about the speed of my driving. Not that I'm fast; the joke is that I'm notoriously slow. If our boys were running late for school they wanted their Mum to drive: "Please Mum, will you take us? If Dad takes us, we'll never get there on time." So you can imagine the hilarity in our home when one day I came home with a speeding ticket!

Some weeks later, I went to driving school. It's a strange experience, arriving with a group of people (none of whom want to be there), shuffling into a classroom, and trying not to be noticed. But noticed I was. During the coffee break, a woman who evidently had visited our church came across the room toward me. "You're Pastor Colin, aren't you? I didn't expect to see *you* here!"

No one goes to driving school with joy. It's a form of penance: a miserable experience that will reinforce the reality that you have done wrong and restrain you from repeating the same offense in the future. Repentance is very different from penance. It is not a path of misery but a path of joy.

Jesus came into the world to announce good news. "The Spirit of the Lord is upon me, because he has anointed me to proclaim good news to the poor" (Luke 4:18). "I must preach the good news of the kingdom of God," He said, "for I was sent for this purpose" (4:43).

What was this good news?

When Matthew introduces the public ministry of Jesus, he tells us that "Jesus began to preach, saying, 'Repent, for the kingdom of heaven is at hand'" (Matthew 4:17).

Notice that "repent" is the first word of God's good news! Real and lasting change is possible because God has come near to you in Jesus Christ. So, if you think of repentance as beating up on yourself, please think again. The hidden path we are describing in this book is not a miserable journey of self-condemnation and regret. Repentance brings joy in heaven, and as you pursue this hidden path, you will find joy in it too.

A second misunderstanding of repentance is to think of it as a one-off event at the beginning of the Christian life when you admit that you are a sinner and tell God you are sorry.

If you grew up hearing the ABCs of the gospel ("Admit you are a sinner. Believe in the Lord Jesus Christ. Commit to following Him.") it would be natural for you to assume that repenting is something you did a long time ago. And so you might be inclined to say, "Been there. Done that."

Repentance is more than a gateway to the Christian life. It is a journey that lasts a lifetime. This is one of the great truths that the Reformers rediscovered in the Bible. The first of Martin Luther's Ninety-Five Theses said, "When our Lord and Master, Jesus Christ, said 'Repent,' He called for the entire life of believers to be one of repentance." John Calvin also understood repentance as a continuing journey and criticized those who "limit to a paltry few days a repentance that, for a Christian man, ought to extend throughout his life."[1]

Repentance is a continuing journey in which you become more like Jesus, and God's plan is that your repentance should deepen as you grow in your Christian life. When you grasp the true meaning of repentance, you will have the joy of discovering that it is the hidden path to a transformed life.

REPENTANCE DEEPENS OVER TIME

Some years ago, I came across a definition of repentance in the writings of J. I. Packer that I have found extremely helpful:

> Repentance means turning
> from as much as you know of your sin
> to give as much as you know of yourself
> to as much as you know of your God.[2]

Let's take a closer look at this definition.

Turning from as Much as you Know of Your Sin

As you grow in the Christian life you will be more conscious of sin than you were before. This is counterintuitive. It would be natural for us to expect that as Christians mature they have less concern over sin in their lives. But the opposite is the case.

You discovered that you were a sinner when you became a Christian, but as the Holy Spirit continues to shine the light of truth into your life, you see more clearly what needs to change. The more light you have, the more sin you see.

If you are growing as a Christian, you will be more conscious of sin in your life now than you used to be. Don't be dismayed by this. A growing awareness of the sins hiding in your heart is a sign of progress. It is irrefutable evidence that the Holy Spirit is at work in your life.

God, in His mercy, reveals our sins to us slowly. If God were to show you the full extent of every sin lurking in your heart, you would be completely devastated. So God shows us what needs to change in our lives slowly. He reveals the sins hiding in our hearts, not with a floodlight but with a flashlight.

As you grow in your Christian life you will become more aware of hidden sins lurking in your heart. And for this reason, your repentance will deepen over time.

Giving as Much as You Know of Yourself

When you became a Christian, you gave your life to Jesus. But as you grow, you will find there are areas of your life that need to be surrendered more fully to Him. Life is a journey of self-discovery, and your repentance will deepen as you come to a fuller knowledge of yourself.

To as Much as You Know of Your God

When you became a Christian, you came to know God. But as you mature in your faith, you will come to know Him more deeply—and as you know more of God, your repentance will deepen.

Repentance, at its heart, is about knowing God, leaving sin, and giving yourself. And as you come to know more of God, more of your sin, and more of yourself, your repentance will deepen.

A MAP FOR OUR JOURNEY

Before you begin a journey, it is wise to plan your route, especially if you are traveling on unmarked roads, where it is easy to miss a turn and find yourself lost.

The journey to a transformed life begins with finding where the hidden path lies, and the focus of our first three chapters will be on finding this path. Using Packer's definition as a framework, we will learn what repentance is and discover how to pursue it with joy. Chapter 1 will focus on growing in your knowledge of God, chapter 2 on turning more fully from your sin, and chapter 3 on giving yourself more deeply to God.

The last three chapters will explore the transformed life. Chapter 4 will describe what it looks like to pursue the path of repentance. We will look at the difference between repentance and regret, and identify some distinguishing marks of true repentance. As you pursue this path there may be times when you wonder if you are making any progress, so chapter 5 will offer some encouragement to keep you pressing on. And in chapter 6, we will end where we began—with the joy of repentance and the motivating power of the love of God.

Real and lasting change is possible for you through faith in Jesus Christ. The hidden path of repentance leads to a transformed life, and however hard this path may be for you, Jesus Christ will walk with you on it.

So don't settle for telling yourself, "This is just how I am. I've always been like this. I'll never be different." You can grow. You can change. You can make progress.

Don't expect this journey to be easy. Jesus said, "Enter by the narrow gate. . . . For the gate is narrow and the way is hard that leads to life, and those who find it are few" (Matthew 7:13–14). The path of repentance can be hard to navigate, and sometimes your progress may be slow. So why choose this path? Because, Jesus says, it "leads to life."

My aim in this book is to encourage you in your pursuit of repentance and to help you see how the hidden path leads to a transformed life. As you learn more about God, more about your sin, and more about yourself, your repentance will deepen, your joy will increase, and you will grow in likeness to Jesus.

KNOWING GOD

If someone were to ask you how to repent, how would you answer? You might suggest that they take a careful look at their lives, identify some things that are displeasing to God, confess these as sin, ask for God's forgiveness, and then watch carefully to resist the return of these sins in the future.

That would be a good answer, and we will look at this dimension of repentance in the next chapter. But the place to begin in repentance is not with listing your sins but with knowing God. Mike Mason says it well: "For the disciple of Jesus . . . the ongoing work of repentance is not so much a sign of sin as it is of normal, healthy spiritual growth."[1]

Repentance is more than being sorry for your sins. It is,

in J. I. Packer's helpful definition, "turning from as much as you know of your sin to give as much as you know of yourself *to as much as you know of your God.*" [2]

There are three areas of growth here: turning from sin, understanding yourself, and knowing God. So thinking of repentance only in terms of abandoning sin severely limits its scope and misses much of its joy.

WHY WOULD A BLAMELESS MAN REPENT?

The book of Job begins with God commending His servant as a "blameless and upright man" (Job 1:8), and it ends with God commending Job again. Unlike his misguided friends, Job spoke "what is right" about God (42:7, 8). So why would the last words of this blameless man be "I despise myself, and *repent* in dust and ashes" (42:6, italics added)?

The question is a puzzling one for two reasons. First, throughout the book Job maintained that he was not hiding a secret sin, despite the persistent accusations of his friends. And second, at no time in the entire story did God ever accuse Job of sin. And yet the story ends with this godly man repenting. Clearly there is more to repentance than turning from known sin. So let's take a closer look at this story.

Job was the godliest man of his generation. God said, "there is none like him on the earth, a blameless and upright man, who fears God and turns away from evil" (1:8). But one day, the bottom fell out of Job's life. His servants and animals were attacked and killed by a gang called the Sabeans (1:14–15). Fire fell from heaven, burning up his sheep (1:16). A messenger came with the report that three raiding parties had taken Job's camels and put his servants to the sword (1:17). Then, most devastating of all, Job received news that a great wind had struck a house where his sons and daughters had gathered. The house had collapsed, and all Job's children were dead (1:18–19).

It is hard to imagine a greater disaster coming to one man in a single day. Job lost his flocks, his servants, and his entire family. And this was only the beginning of Job's suffering. What followed was an intense battle in which Job struggled with himself, with his friends, and, most of all, with God.

Job's friends were convinced his suffering was a consequence of a hidden sin in his life, and they felt sure that the best way to help him was to urge him to come clean and tell them what it was.

Job was a rich and powerful man. Perhaps he had denied justice to someone with whom he traded? Perhaps he had been indifferent to the needs of the poor? Perhaps he had indulged in some secret sexual sin? Job's friends felt sure that they would find something if they kept digging. But Job maintained his innocence and, after hearing all of their questions, went through a catalog of sins, calling down judgments on himself if he were guilty of any of them:

- If I have walked with falsehood . . . (31:5)
- If my heart has been enticed toward a woman . . . (31:9)
- If I have withheld anything that the poor desired . . . (31:16)
- If I have seen anyone perish for lack of clothing . . . (31:19)
- If I have raised my hand against the fatherless . . . (31:21)
- If I have made gold my trust . . . (31:24)
- If I have rejoiced at the ruin of him who hated me . . . (31:29)
- If I have concealed my transgressions as others do by hiding my iniquity in my heart . . . (31:33)

The repeated *if* shows that Job was saying, "But I didn't do any of these things!" Job insisted that he was not covering up a secret sin. Having looked honestly at his own life, he was not aware of anything that would explain what he had endured. Job's suffering remained a mystery to him, and he refused to accept the trite assumption of his friends that he was suffering on account of a hidden sin.

What Job wanted was a chance to ask God some honest questions.

Oh, that I knew where I might find him,
     that I might come even to his seat!
  I would lay my case before him
     and fill my mouth with arguments. (23:3–4)

Job felt sure that if he had the opportunity to present his case, God would listen. And when He answered, Job felt sure he would understand whatever God had to say (23:5).

At the end of the book, Job got what he wanted. He experienced a remarkable encounter in which God appeared to him and spoke to him directly (Job 38–41). But instead of listening while Job presented his case, God took the initiative and asked Job multiple questions. "Dress for action like a man," God said, "I will question you" (38:3):

- Where were you when I laid the foundation of the earth? (38:4)
- Who determined its measurements—surely you know! Or who stretched the line upon it? (38:4–5)
- On what were its bases sunk, or who laid its cornerstone when . . . all the sons of God shouted for joy? (38:6–7)
- Have you commanded the morning since your days began, and caused the dawn to know its place? (38:12)
- Have you entered into the springs of the sea, or walked in the recesses of the deep? (38:16)
- Have you entered the storehouses of the snow, or have you seen the storehouses of the hail? (38:22)
- Can you send forth lightnings, that they may go and say to you, "Here we are"? (38:35).

Job could not answer any of these questions. Instead of bringing his case before God, Job said,

Behold, I am of small account; what shall I answer you?
        I lay my hand on my mouth.
I have spoken once, and I will not answer;
        twice, but I will proceed no further. (40:3–5)

22

Then, after God had spoken to him a second time, Job said,

I have uttered what I did not understand,
> things too wonderful for me, which I did not know . . .
I had heard of you by the hearing of the ear,
> but now my eye sees you;
therefore I despise myself,
> and *repent* in dust and ashes. (42:3–6 italics added)

Job repented, not because he was convicted of some secret or hidden sin but because he saw God's glory as he had never seen it before.

THE TRANSFORMING POWER OF WORSHIP

Job was a strong believer, but his faith had been stretched to the limit by what he suffered. He believed in God, but he also had questions for God, and he had called on God to answer these questions: "Hear, and I will speak; I will question you" (42:4).

You may also come to a place where you have more questions than answers and your faith is stretched to the limit. Most Christians have been there, but no Christian

23

wants to stay there. So how did Job move from questioning God to worshiping God?

The breakthrough in Job's life came when he got a fresh glimpse of God's greatness and glory. Coming to know God more deeply led Job to worship, and worship changed him.

Job saw that God was far greater and more glorious than he had grasped before. He realized that there were more mysteries in God's vast universe than he could ever comprehend and that his questions were just a tiny fraction of what he did not know.

Job had been trying to make sense of his suffering, but when he saw the glory of God, he repented. Repentance involves turning to as much as you know of God, and the more you see of God's glory, the deeper your repentance will become.

Our quest in this book is to find the hidden path to a transformed life. *Transformed* is a strong word that holds a big promise, and I would not have used it if it were not in the Bible. Paul speaks of how believers "are being "transformed into the same image [i.e., the image of Christ] from one degree of glory to another" (2 Corinthians 3:18).

Notice, first, that Paul is describing a gradual process: we "*are being* transformed from one degree of glory to another." Growth takes place over time, so no Christian should expect instantaneous transformation. But God is committed to making us like Christ, and the word He uses to describe that change is *transformed*.

The big question, of course, is how? How can I be transformed into the same image from one degree of glory to another? Paul says, "We all, with unveiled face, *beholding the glory of the Lord* are being transformed into the same image" (3:18, italics added). We become more like Jesus by beholding more of His glory.

John tells us that when Christ appears, "we shall be like him, because we shall see him as he is" (1 John 3:2). Your transformation will be complete when your faith is turned to sight and you see Christ face to face. Until then, the more you come to know Him, the more you will be like Him.

FINDING COMFORT IN WORSHIP

Charles Spurgeon noted that the Hebrew word translated in

Job 42:6 as "repent" is also used in other places in the Old Testament to express comfort:

> [Isaac] took Rebekah, and she became his wife, and he loved her. So Isaac was *comforted* after his mother's death. (Genesis 24:67, italics added)

The word translated "comforted" in Genesis 24 is the same word that Job used to say, "I repent."

That might seem odd to you as it did, at first, to me. How can the same word be translated as "repent" and "comfort"? Surely these are two very different things? But as we have seen, there is joy in repentance, so perhaps it not surprising to find that there is comfort in it too.

Job's response to the unveiled glory of God could be translated as:

I had heard of you by the hearing of the ear,
　　　but now my eye sees you;
therefore I despise myself,
　　　and *find comfort* in dust and ashes. (Job 42:5–6, italics added)

Why would Job find "comfort" in dust and ashes? The Bible tells us that we're made from dust, that we'll return to dust, and that God remembers we are dust (Genesis 2:7, 3:19, Psalm 103:14). So dust reminds us of who we are.

Sometimes we forget that we are dust, and that was Job's problem. He felt God owed him an explanation, and he thought he would be able to understand if God gave it to him (Job 23:5). But when God spoke, the tables were turned. God asked all the questions, and Job was stunned into silence.

When Job was given a greater glimpse of the glory of God, he was finally able to live with his unresolved questions and set aside his bitter complaints—and, to someone who loved God, that brought tremendous relief. Job had been carrying the burden of a strain in the relationship that mattered most in his life, and he had found it exhausting: "Today also my complaint is bitter; my hand is heavy on account of my groaning" (23:2).

Job's language here is similar to David's when he described the weight of living with unconfessed sin: "When I kept silent, my bones wasted away through my groaning all day long. . . . My strength was dried up as by the heat of summer" (Psalm 32:3–4). Unresolved conflicts with God have the same effect as unconfessed sin. Both are exhausting. And repentance brought comfort to Job because it resolved his conflict with God. Job remembered that he is dust, and this brought him tremendous relief.

Perhaps, like Job, you know what it is for painful experiences to place a strain on your relationship with God and make you a questioner rather than a worshiper of God. As long as you are out of sorts with God, you cannot have peace. But if you saw more of His glory, you would experience tremendous relief.

It's easy to get the idea that we should know all things, control all things, and shape all things. But the secret things belong to God (Deuteronomy 29:29). Prying into what God has kept secret will tear you apart. Submitting to Him will bring you comfort and peace.

If Job could comfort himself with dust and ashes, so can you. Come humbly to God and tell Him, "I don't need to know all the mysteries of life. It is enough for me to know that You reign over all things, that You have made me, and that when this body returns to dust, I will be with You forever."

You will find great comfort in confessing with Job, "I have uttered what I did not understand, things too wonderful for me, which I did not know" (Job 42:3), and with David, when he said, "O Lord, my heart is not lifted up; my eyes are not raised too high; I do not occupy myself with things too great and too marvelous for me. But I have calmed and quieted my soul, like a weaned child with its mother" (Psalm 131:1–2).

HOW TO DEEPEN YOUR WORSHIP

The story of Job shows us that lasting change begins with deeper worship. So how can you, like Job, come to know God more deeply? First by asking and second by looking.

Despite all his pain, Job kept seeking after God. It was the same with Moses, who said to God: "Please show me your glory" (Exodus 33:18). When you see that comfort is found in knowing God more deeply, you will want to see more of His glory too.

Don't stop gathering with other believers for worship because you have questions. Worship will deepen your knowledge of God and bring you comfort. So ask God to open your eyes to His glory as you sing, read, pray, and hear the preaching of the Word: "Open my eyes, that I may behold wondrous things out of your law" (Psalm 119:18). Make this your prayer every time you come to worship.

Then, as you ask God to help you see, look! As we saw earlier, it is by *"beholding* the glory of the Lord," that we are "transformed into the same image from one degree of glory to another" (2 Corinthians 3:18, italics added).

The Bible uses *beholding* (or *looking*) as another way of speaking about believing. Job experienced a remarkable revelation of the glory of God, but we have something better. God has taken flesh and come into our world in the person of Jesus Christ. John says, "We have seen his glory, glory as of the only Son from the Father, full of grace and truth" (John 1:14). Jesus is "the radiance of the glory of God," (Hebrews 1:3), and we see "the light of the knowledge of the glory of God in the face of Jesus Christ" (2 Corinthians 4:6).

So if you want to see the glory of the Lord, look at Jesus Christ. See His compassion—embracing children in His arms, weeping with a grieving family at the grave of a dear friend, touching a leper no one else would go near. Look at His authority—confronting those who abused power in His temple, casting out demons from a distraught man, and breathing on His disciples, saying, "Receive the Holy Spirit" and "As the Father has sent me, even so I am sending you" (John 20:21–22).

Look at Jesus in His greatest work—dying on the cross as the sacrifice for your sins, rising from the dead so that you could have everlasting life, and ascending into heaven to represent you before the Father. This is your God! So look! And ask yourself, "What is there about Jesus that I cannot trust? What is there in Him that I cannot love?"

Build the habit of asking and looking into your life. Set a pattern in which you open the Bible and ask God to open your eyes (Psalm 119:18). Then look into God's Word and ask yourself, "What do I learn about God here today? How will believing this change me?"

Job's repentance was a journey in which he moved from being a believer who questioned to a believer who worshiped. And this journey was made not because Job's questions were answered but because he came to know God more deeply. Job found the hidden path to a transformed life by knowing God more deeply, and his journey can be yours.

LEAVING SIN

Imagine living in a remote village where there are many dangers, especially from wild animals. One night, a leopard slips into the village and takes the life of a child. The leopard then retreats into the jungle, but having the taste of blood, it will soon be back for more. For the safety of the village, the leopard must be hunted and killed.

The village chief asks for volunteers, and you step forward. Taking your spear in hand, you move out into the bush looking for signs of the leopard's presence. You walk slowly because you know that while you are stalking the leopard, the leopard is stalking you. You are the hunter, but you are also the hunted. A deadly confrontation is inevitable: either you will kill the leopard, or the leopard will kill you.

God uses the image of a wild animal intent on destruction to warn us of sin's power: "Sin is crouching at the door. Its desire is contrary to you, but you must rule over it" (Genesis 4:7). Sin lurks at the door of your life—ready to pounce and destroy. If you ignore it, sin will creep up on you, and if it gets hold of you, it will not want to let go. So God says you must "rule over it," and that means you must find it, confront it, and subdue it.

Temptations of various kinds will keep coming at you, and when you gain the upper hand in one area of your life, sin will come at you in another. The scene of the battle may change, but the conflict never ends.

A LANDING PLACE FOR SIN

Suppose you are living on a small island that belongs to a kind and generous king. Enemies invade the island, and you are taken captive. One day the king comes with his army and sets you free. The island is liberated, and you enjoy the blessing of living under the king's rule. But somewhere on the island there is a hidden landing, and every night enemies arrive to continue their work of sabotage and subversion.

Sinclair Ferguson pictures temptation coming toward us like a plane looking for a place to land: "The enemies we face attack us from outside our own hearts and move inward . . . to draw our affections towards themselves and away from our Lord. But their power rests on a further factor, namely the 'landing ground' they are able to find within our own lives."[1]

Our flesh provides a landing place for sin. "The desires of the flesh are against the Spirit, and the desires of the Spirit are against the flesh, for these are opposed to each other" (Galatians 5:17). When you became a Christian, the guilt of your sin was forgiven, and the condemnation of your sin was removed. But the root of sin remains in your life, and that is why, as long as you are in the body, you will have to fight against temptation.

The "desires of the flesh" are inclinations and impulses of the heart that are offensive to God and destructive to us. They include pride, greed, envy, anger, laziness, lust, and gluttony, which are sometimes referred to as the seven deadly sins. None of these are actions; all of them are impulses or inclinations, and this is where our greatest battles are fought. This impulse to sin remains in your flesh, and you have a lifelong battle on your hands.

James tells us that "each person is tempted when he is lured and enticed *by his own desire*" (James 1:14, italics added). The temptations we face are tied to our own flesh, and that means your battles are, to some extent, rooted in your temperament. All Christians are tempted, but we are not tempted in the same ways. David was an impulsive person, and his temptation with Bathsheba was a spur-of-the-moment decision. Jonah was an introvert, and his sulking outside Nineveh reflected his tendency to retreat into himself. Hezekiah was an extrovert, and his temptation to show his treasures to a visiting king reflected his desire to make a good impression.

A person who is meticulous may be tempted to hold a grudge and not to forgive, and a person who is naturally cautious may be tempted to hold back in fear when they should launch out in faith. So become a student of your own heart and get to know the particular temptations that come with your temperament. Are you the kind of person who might be tempted to control, or to withdraw? Are you prone to resent, or to rebel? Knowing what you are up against will help you to guard against it.

KNOW IT!

As you come to know God better, you will become more aware of hidden sins in your life. This will be discouraging, and you may sometimes wonder if you are a Christian at all: "Can I really belong to Christ when I struggle with sin like this?"

The good news is that awareness of your own sin is not a sign of failure; it is a sign of progress. Repentance, as we have seen, is *turning from as much as you know of your sin to give as much as you know of yourself to as much as you know of your God.* So knowing your own sins is essential to moving forward on the path of repentance. Can you name two or three sins that pose the greatest threat to you right now? If not, how can you guard against them? To progress further, you must identify your primary battles.

So how can you identify the sins that hide in your heart? God says that His Word is "a lamp to [your] feet and a light to [your] path" (Psalm 119:105), so use the light of Scripture to expose the hidden sins of your heart. Ask of any passage of Scripture: "Is there a sin here to avoid?"

Pose Questions to Yourself

In the last chapter, we saw that Job rehearsed a catalog of sins, arguing that he was not guilty of any of them. He said, "[If] my heart has gone after my eyes . . . if I have withheld anything that the poor desired . . . if I have rejoiced at the ruin of him who hated me . . ." (Job 31:7, 16, 29).

But we may not be as blameless as Job, and I found it helpful to turn Job's words into questions that I could pose to myself: "Has my heart gone after my eyes? Have I withheld something that the poor desired? Have I been secretly happy when trouble came to someone who opposed me?"

Turn Virtues on Their Heads

When you see a virtue described in Scripture, turn it on its head and ask yourself if you are guilty of the opposite. To take another example, when you read "Love is patient and kind; love does not envy or boast; it is not arrogant or rude. It does not insist on its own way; it is not irritable or resentful" (1 Corinthians 13:4–5), ask yourself, "Where am I being impatient? Is there someone to whom I have been unkind? Who do I envy? Where am I insisting on my own way? Have I become irritable or resentful?" If you find any of these impulses in your soul, confess them as sin to God and ask the Lord to forgive you and to help you show patience and kindness instead.

One benefit of using the Scripture in this way is that you are inviting God to shine His light on the things you need to see. Over time, you will find that your reading of Scripture becomes like a conversation in which the Holy Spirit shows you what needs to change in your life.

Learn from Good and Bad Examples
Reading the story of the four men who wanted to bring their paralyzed friend to Jesus, I was struck by the sheer determination of these men. When they arrived at the house where Jesus was teaching, they could not get near to the Savior because of the crowd. Instead of giving up, they

climbed on the roof, dug a hole, and then lowered their friend on his mattress so that he arrived right in front of Jesus (Mark 2:1–12). When I asked the question "Is there a sin here to avoid?" I saw the sin of giving up too quickly, and immediately my mind went to a difficult situation in which I was close to throwing in the towel. God spoke to me through that, and I found new strength to persevere.

You can uncover hidden sins by identifying commands you have not obeyed, promises you have not believed, examples you have not followed, and warnings you have ignored. God can use any part of His Word to shine His light into the hidden recesses of your heart. And when you learn to use the Scripture in self-examination, you will begin to see what you are up against.

STALK IT!

Let's return to the story of the leopard. You know that the leopard is a threat to the village and that, having tasted blood, it will soon be back for more. So you don't wait around for the leopard to return. You go out and hunt it. And the same is true of sin.

Stalking, or hunting, is the process by which you track something down, and stalking sin means getting into a position where you can see the movements of a particular sin in your life. Once you know what you are looking for, you must get it in your sights—and then you can take action against it.

Note Your Most Vulnerable Times

You can stalk sin, first, by noting the times when you are most vulnerable to its activity. Jesus told His disciples to "watch and pray" (Matthew 26:41). He gave this command when they were tired. The disciples had walked close to a hundred miles from Galilee to Jerusalem, and their time there was filled with relentless demands. By the time they arrived in the Garden of Gethsemane, late at night, they were exhausted. When we are tired, we don't see things clearly. I know that is true of me. When I am tired, I am less careful with what I say, less patient with other people, and more easily provoked. When you are tired you will be more vulnerable to temptation, so watch and pray.

Jesus told His disciples to "watch and pray" after Judas, who had been the disciples' friend and colleague for three years, had walked out of the upper room. When a friend or loved one falls into sin or abandons the faith, you will be especially vulnerable to temptation. What they have done gets into your mind, and something within you may say, "If he can do that, why shouldn't I?" When Paul directs mature believers to gently restore a brother or sister who has been trapped by a particular sin, he says, "Keep watch on yourself, lest you too be tempted" (Galatians 6:1). It would be a great tragedy if in seeking to restore someone from sin you yourself fell into the same temptation that had trapped them.

Jesus counseled His disciples to "watch and pray" when hostility was brewing. It was one thing for the disciples to be identified with Jesus on Palm Sunday when all of the crowds were cheering, but it was a different story on Good Friday when the crowds were calling for Him to be crucified. As our culture becomes increasingly hostile to Jesus, we need to watch and pray that we may not enter into temptation.

When are you most vulnerable to temptation? When you are anonymous? When you are online? When you are with friends? After a big success? Note the times and circumstances so that when they come you can be especially on your guard.

Learn from Your Past Experience

A second way to stalk sin is to learn from your past experience. Good teams get better by carefully reviewing past failures. A football team will analyze, in detail, every touchdown they have given up, so that they can develop a better strategy: Where were we exposed? Why did that happen? How can we do better next time?

In the same way, you can grow in your ability to withstand temptation by learning from your failures. Looking honestly at your past defeats may sound discouraging, but as you study where you have failed in the past, you will learn how to succeed in the future. John Owen says, "This is how men deal with their enemies. They search out their plans, ponder their goals, and consider how, and by what means they have prevailed over them *in the past*. Then they can be defeated."[2]

If you can list the factors that contributed to your falling into temptation last time, you will have the wisdom you need to face the same temptation next time it comes.

Consider Where Sin Would Lead You

A third way to stalk sin is to consider where sin would lead you. Sin begins in small ways, with a desire that might seem pretty harmless, but "desire when it has conceived gives birth to sin, and sin when it is fully grown brings forth death" (James 1:15). So when you face what may seem like a small temptation, ask yourself where this temptation would lead you *if you followed it all the way.*

John Owen gives this wise counsel: "Ask envy what it aims at. Murder and destruction are its natural conclusion."[3] A little bit of envy may not seem like a big deal, but the heart of envy is wanting for yourself what God has given to someone else. And if you followed that impulse all the way to its natural conclusion, it would lead you to murder. That little envious thought carries the seed of murder, so resist it as vigorously as you would resist the thought of taking another person's life.

In a similar vein, Owen says, "Every unclean thought or glance would be adultery if it could. Every covetous desire would be oppression and every unbelieving thought would be atheism. . . . Sin's expression is modest in the beginning, but, once it has gained a foothold, it continues to take further ground and presses on to greater heights."[4]

When you feel an impulse to sin, trace its trajectory. Take a good look at where it would lead you if you followed it all the way, and resist the first thought as strongly as you would the ultimate destination.

KILL IT!

Returning again to the story of the leopard, you first recognized the danger the leopard presented, and then you went out to find it. But the story does not end there. There is one more thing to do: you must kill the leopard before the leopard kills you. As John Owen puts it, "always be killing sin or it will be killing you."[5]

Killing sin is the language of Scripture:

> If you live according to the flesh you will die, but if by the Spirit you *put to death* the deeds of the body, you will live. (Romans 8:13, italics added)

> *Put to death* therefore what is earthly in you: sexual immorality, impurity, passion, evil desire, and covetousness, which is idolatry. (Colossians 3:5, italics added)

> Those who belong to Christ Jesus have *crucified* the flesh with its passions and desires. (Galatians 5:24, italics added)

Crucifixion is a slow death, so when Paul says that we have "crucified the flesh," this means that the flesh is dying, not that it is dead. John Brown says helpfully, "Crucifixion . . . produced death not suddenly but gradually. . . . True Christians . . . do not succeed in completely destroying it [that is, the flesh] while here below; but they have fixed it to the cross, and they are determined to keep it there till it expire."[6]

Sinclair Ferguson gives a clear description of what this involves:

> What then is this killing sin? It is a constant battle against sin which we fight daily—the refusal to allow the eye to wander, the mind to contemplate, the affections to run after anything which will draw us from Christ. It is the deliberate rejection of any sinful

thought, suggestion, desire, aspiration, deed, circumstance or provocation at the moment we become conscious of its existence. It is the constant endeavor to do all in our powers to weaken the grip which sin in general, and its manifestations in our own lives in particular, has. . . . It is by resolutely weeding the garden of the heart, and also by planting, watering and nurturing Christian graces there, that putting sin to death will take place.[7]

Killing sin is a continuing battle in which we refuse to give ground to sin and seek, by God's grace, to grow in godliness instead. John Owen says that mortification (putting sin to death) involves "a habitual weakening of sin."[8] Every time you say yes to a temptation you increase its power in your life, and every time you say no to a temptation you weaken its power over you.

The good news is that, by God's grace, you will make progress. But how do you measure progress in your battle against sin? What does success look like in a warfare that will continue for the rest of your life?

You are making progress in your battle with sin when the sin that once had mastery over you is gradually and increasingly subdued so that its assault is less frequent and less intense, and that you do not give way as easily as you did in the past. The sin that tempts you has not been eradicated, but it has been weakened, and it no longer has the power it once had over you.

So now that you know your primary battles and have a clear view of what you are up against, here is the next question: What can you do to make progress in subduing the power of sin in your life?

Start Immediately

Develop the habit of resisting sin at its first approach. When a thought or impulse to sin comes to your mind, reject it immediately. Give it no quarter.

When a salesman comes to your door, it is not difficult to say, "Sorry, but I'm not interested." But if you invite him in and listen as he tells you how much you need what he is selling and how much better your life will be when you have it, your mind and heart will become engaged. Then it will be much harder to say no.

The longer you allow a sin to grow in your life, the harder

your battle to get free from it will be. Like weeds in a garden, the longer a sin is left, the deeper its roots will be.

Perhaps, at this point, you are feeling that you should have taken up the fight against a particular temptation years ago. But you didn't, and now your heart is heavy because you know that the battle you face will be intense.

Getting free from the power of habit formed over many years will not be easy, so let me give you this encouragement: the longer you have indulged a particular sin, the more urgent it is that you begin your battle against it now. Last week, last year, or perhaps even ten or twenty years ago would have been better, but these opportunities have gone. God gives you today, and delaying longer will only make the problem worse.

God's grace is sufficient for you to prevail in this battle, so begin it today. John Owen says, "By faith ponder this, that though you are in no way able to conquer your own disordered state, and though you are weary of fighting against it . . . there is enough in Jesus Christ to give you relief."[9]

Keep at It

Our struggle against the flesh is a long warfare, and you will not win this war by one prayer, one commitment, or one act of faith. But if, by the power of the Holy Spirit, you offer sustained and continued resistance to every approach of sin, you will, over time, prevail.

So win some battles in your war against the flesh. Notice I didn't say "win *the* battle," because the conflict will continue throughout your life. But you can and will win some battles. And as you do, sin will become weaker, and you, by God's grace, will become stronger.

Move the Ball Forward

In these pages, we have pictured our conflict with sin in terms of hunting an animal, weeding a garden, and fighting a battle. I've also found it helpful to picture this conflict as a drive in a game of football. In any game there will be times when you are on offense and times when you are playing defense. But at its heart, football is about moving the ball forward.

This picture reminds me that even when we are gaining yards in a drive, we can never rest. When you think that you are doing well, sin can intercept the ball and be down in the end zone before you know it. So be careful when you think you are making progress.

And remember to have your defense ready when you have put points on the board. If you have been blessed in serving, if you have led someone to Christ, or if your ministry is expanding, watch out: sin will be coming back at you.

There will be times when sin breaks through your defense and scores a touchdown. This is not the time for you to quit. It is time for you to begin a new drive against that sin in your life. Look your sin in the face and say,

Rejoice not over me, O my enemy;
      when I fall, I shall rise;
when I sit in darkness,
      the LORD will be a light to me. (Micah 7:8)

Make Sure You Are in Christ
When Paul sets out our calling to deal decisively with sin

in our lives, he says, "Put to death *therefore* what is earthly in you" (Colossians 3:5, italics added). Notice the word "therefore." What is it there for? Clearly, it refers back to what Paul has just been saying, which is that believers have been raised to new life with Christ and that our lives have been hidden with Christ in God (3:1, 3).

When you are in Christ, you have power. Sin will always be your enemy, but it is no longer your master (Romans 6:14). Before you were sin's prisoner, but now you have been set free, and you are in a position to fight.

Is this true of you? Have you been raised to new life in Christ? If so, the Holy Spirit lives in you, and "*by the Spirit* you [can] put to death the deeds of the body" (Romans 8:13, italics added). But if you have not yet found this new life, your first and greatest need is to come in faith to Jesus and place your life in His hands.

Jesus died on the cross to reconcile sinners to God, so ask Him to do that for you. He lives so that those who come to Him should no longer be slaves of sin, so ask Him to empower you by His Holy Spirit for the battle that lies ahead. Believe in Him and trust Him to do what you ask. Then you will be in a position to start knowing, stalking, and killing your sins.

GIVING YOURSELF

Repentance, as we have seen, involves turning from sin, but it also involves turning to God and giving yourself to Him. When Paul preached the gospel in Thessalonica, those who believed "turned to God from idols to serve the living and true God" (1 Thessalonians 1:9). These people abandoned what they used to worship and gave themselves to serving the Lord.

Repentance involves both a "turning from" and a "turning to." It is, as we have seen, turning from all that you know of your sin. But there's more. Repentance is *giving all that you know of yourself to God*. There's more here than giving up old sins. God calls us to a life of love that will honor Him, and repentance embraces this new life with joy.

In response to God's grace, we are called to "present [our] bodies as a living sacrifice, holy and acceptable to God" (Romans 12:1), and Paul tells us how this is possible: "Do not be conformed to this world, but be transformed *by the renewal of your mind*" (12:2, italics added).

Two things are essential if you are to give yourself fully and freely to God: (1) you must know who you are, and (2) you must know why you are here. Repentance involves giving *as much as you know of yourself* to God, and you will give yourself more fully to God as you discover more about who you are and why you are here.

WHO AM I?

Who am I? The question of identity can be answered in many different ways. Relationally, I am a husband, a father, a grandfather, a son, a brother, and a friend. Vocationally, I am a pastor. By temperament, I am an introvert. The list could go on. But none of these get to the heart of who I am and why I am here, and none of them, *in themselves,* are reasons to give myself to God. It would be perfectly possible to pursue all of these "identities" out of pure self-interest. So why should I give myself to God?

The first thing you need to know about yourself is that "you were *dead* in the trespasses and sins in which you once walked" (Ephesians 2:1–2, italics added). Notice that Paul does not say you were "trapped" in your sins; you were dead.

Aaron Ralston was trapped for 127 hours when his arm was pinned by a rock in a canyon. He kept hoping that someone would come and help him, but no one came. So as a last resort, in an act of extraordinary courage, he cut off his arm to save his life. A man who is trapped in a canyon may be able to find a way out, but a man who is dead in a canyon is in a different position. He cannot move. He cannot feel. He cannot act.

The media team in our church have a mannequin that they have used for setting up the lighting before recording a video. I call the mannequin "Manny," and on one occasion, I brought him onto the platform and preached to him. I called on him to live by the Ten Commandments and the Sermon on the Mount. With great passion, I exhorted him to love the Lord with all his heart and love his neighbor as himself. I explained the gospel to him clearly and told him that God was ready to forgive him, and that he must take the first step toward God. I pleaded with him to repent and believe, but there was no response.

Manny is a remarkably good-looking fellow. He is tall, dark, and smartly dressed. But there's no life in him. He's dead. And that's what God says about us: "You were dead in the trespasses and sins in which you once walked." You were powerless to change your position. You were alienated from God, unresponsive to His Word, and under His wrath. And there was nothing you could do about it.

And yet, you *did* move toward God. You repented. You believed. You made a commitment to follow Jesus. How in the world did that happen? God made you alive in Christ.

> But God, being rich in mercy, because of the great love with which he loved us, even when we were dead in our trespasses, made us alive together with Christ—by grace you have been saved. (Ephesians 2:4–5)

God took the initiative and brought life where it did not exist before. New affections were formed in your soul: you began to love God, trust God, and desire God. New convictions were formed in your mind: you became aware of your sin, and you were drawn to Christ. New desires were formed in your will: you became dissatisfied with the life you had been living, and you chose freely to give your life to Jesus.

What an amazing transformation: You once felt sure that God was against you; now you know that He is for you in Christ. Your old instinct was to hide from God; now you want to seek him. There's a new hunger and thirst for God in your soul. You want more of Him, and you want Him to have more of you. You were dead, and God brought you to life. By grace you have been saved.

Grace is more than God's opening a door and then standing back to see who will come through. An open door is no different from a closed door to a dead man. God did more than make your salvation possible. He saved you. He made you alive with Christ—even when you were dead in transgressions and sins.

Let God Tell You Who You Are

When Paul tells us that we are to present ourselves to God "as those who *have been* brought from death to life" (Romans 6:13, italics added), he is describing a completed work, not a continuing process. However far you still have to go in your journey of faith and repentance, God *has* brought you from death you to life, and you *have been* made alive in Christ. And it is on this basis of what God has done for you in Christ that you are to give yourself to Him.

But when you look at yourself, your first thought may be: "I am such a long way from what God calls me to be. I am a miserable, pathetic, feeble, useless, powerless, no good, apology for a Christian." Maybe you fell into some sin, or perhaps the faster growth and greater maturity of other Christians made you feel that you were failing. Or maybe you were ashamed of your darker thoughts and wondered if you are really a Christian at all.

Let God tell you who you are: you were dead in transgressions and sins, but God has made you alive with Christ. He has brought you from death to life. Of course, you are still a work in progress, and you have a lot more changing to do, but don't lose sight of what God has done in your life already.

Most Christian are familiar with the continuing work of the Holy Spirit in us, in which He makes us more like Jesus. But I find that some are less familiar with the completed work of the Holy Spirit in us, in which He has brought us from death to life.

We feel comfortable saying "God is changing me," but we would hesitate to say "God has changed me." But both are true. If you are in Christ, you are a new creation. God has brought you from death to life.

The New Testament emphasizes repeatedly what God has already done in the life of a believer:

> Therefore, if anyone is in Christ, he is a new creation. The old has passed away; behold, the new *has come*. (2 Corinthians 5:17, italics added)

> I *have been* crucified with Christ. It is no longer I who live, but Christ who lives in me. (Galatians 2:20, italics added)

Do you not know that your body *is* a temple of the Holy Spirit within you, whom you *have* from God? (1 Corinthians 6:19, italics added)

At one time you were darkness, but now *you are* light in the Lord. (Ephesians 5:8, italics added)

For you *have* died, and your life *is* hidden with Christ in God. (Colossians 3:3, italics added)

You *have been* born again, not of perishable seed but of imperishable, through the living and abiding word of God. (1 Peter 1:23, italics added)

When you know who you are, you will offer yourself to God. This is the logic of Scripture:

Your body is a temple of the Holy Spirit. . . . *So glorify God in your body.* (1 Corinthians 6:19–20, italics added)

You are light. . . . [So] *walk as children of light (for the fruit of light is found in all that is good and right and true).* (Ephesians 5:8–9, italics added)

You have been raised with Christ. . . . [So] *set your minds on things that are above, not on things that are on earth.* (Colossians 3:1–2, italics added)

You have been born again. . . . [So] *love one another earnestly from a pure heart* (1 Peter 1:22-23, italics added)

The Christian life is not about pretending to be something you are not. It is about being who you are in Christ. You have been brought from death to life. God has given you new life, and He calls you to offer that life back to Him.

WHY AM I HERE?

If you are to give yourself fully and freely to God, you must know not only who you are but also why you are here.

Why did God bring you from death to life? Paul says, "He died for all, that those who live might no longer live for themselves but for him who for their sake died and was raised" (2 Corinthians 5:15).

Christ died to release you from the misery of living for yourself and to bring you into the joy of living for Him.

If you live for yourself, you have to fill two roles at the same time. On the one hand, you are being served. Someone is living for you, so you are the boss. But on the other hand, the person who is living for you is yourself, so you are also the servant. To live for yourself means that you are always serving and that you are always being served, and because you are both the boss and the servant, you will always be robbing Peter to pay Paul.

If you live for yourself you will often find yourself in the strange position of beating yourself up in order to make yourself happy. The demands you set are the demands you must meet, and so you are always in a conflict. When you look in the mirror and "self the boss" wants to have a more pleasing image, "self the servant" suffers for not being pretty enough. You look at your life, and "self the boss" says you should have accomplished more. So "self the servant" gets beaten up for not working harder.

Then suppose at some point, you say to yourself, "This is no good, I am living for myself and I am not happy. I see that I'm being too hard on myself, so I will lighten up and give myself a break." But here's the problem: you are still not happy because while "self the servant" is let off the hook, "self the boss" is no longer being served!

Living for yourself is an absolute nightmare. Whenever you crack the whip as the master, you feel the lash as the servant. And when you cut some slack on the servant, you end up being shortchanged as the master. You cannot possibly win.

Christ died to deliver you from this misery: "He died for all, that those who live might no longer live for themselves but for him who for their sake died and was raised" (2 Corinthians 5:15). God has brought you from death to life, and the purpose of your new life is to give yourself to God.

GIVE YOURSELF TO GOD AS YOU ARE

Perhaps you would like to offer yourself to God, but don't feel that you have much to give. If your life is not as you would want it to be, you are in good company.

Take the Story of Joseph

He was a gifted man, and God had great purposes for his life. Joseph knew from the vision God gave him that he had been called to a special ministry.

But what happened to him? He was beaten up by his brothers and left for dead in a pit. Traveling traders found him and sold him as a slave in Egypt, where he worked hard with great integrity. But he ended up in prison because false accusations were made against him.

Put yourself in Joseph's shoes. I'm sure I would have been saying to God, *If You have a great purpose for my life, why am I here? Where's Your plan in all of this? What use can I be to You in a prison cell?*

But Joseph gave himself to God in the prison. He exercised faith, pursued integrity, and ministered to the men God had placed next to him.

Then God stepped in and Joseph was used to save his entire family.

Take the Story of Moses

He was a gifted leader with a vision for the people of God. What happened to him? He was betrayed by his own people, and he found himself looking after sheep in the desert (Exodus 3:1).

Put yourself in Moses' shoes. I'm sure I would have been saying to God, *You gave me a vision for Your people, so why am I here? Where's Your plan in all of this? What kind of ministry can I have in this wilderness?*

But Moses gave himself to God in the desert. He honored God in his work as a shepherd. Then God stepped in and made Moses the shepherd of His people.

Do you see the principle? Give yourself to God in your present circumstances, however limited they may be, and God will work our His purpose in your life.

Perhaps you are thinking, "I could be useful to God if only my circumstances were different: If only I didn't suffer from this illness. If only I had a more committed spouse. If only . . ."

Or perhaps you feel that one day you will be able to give yourself to God more fully: "One day when I don't have the pressure of my present work. One day when my children are no longer at home. One day when I have resolved the problems that currently dominate my life."

Or perhaps you feel that you can offer yourself when you

have more faith or when you have traveled farther on the road to repentance or when you have more wisdom or when you have more peace.

Don't fall into the trap of thinking that you can only be useful to God when you are in a better place. You are not yet as you want to be or as you will be, but God calls you to give yourself to Him right now—just as you are.

The only life you can offer to God is the life that God has given to you. So, offer yourself to God as you are, where you are, and leave the outcome in His hands. God knows what He will do with you. Your calling is to give yourself to Him as one who is wholly available right now—whatever your circumstances.

GIVE YOURSELF TO GOD IN ALL THAT YOU DO

Someone may say, "I would like to give myself to God, but my life is full. I don't have margin, and so there's not much that I can offer."

Take a step back from your busy schedule and consider the life of an ordinary person. She has 24 hours in the day.

Now let's suppose that she spends 8 hours sleeping, and that she spends another 8 hours at work. With breakfast, lunch, and dinner she spends 3 hours eating. And if she has a 1-hour commute, she spends another 2 hours traveling to and from work. That leaves 3 hours, of which she might give 2 to her friends and family, which leaves her with just 1 hour available in the day.

If giving yourself to God means giving that single hour, then what she can offer would only be a very small part of her life. That's clearly not what Paul has in mind when he says, "Present yourselves to God" (Romans 6:13).

Giving yourself to God means *offering the whole of your life*. That includes the sleeping, the eating, the working, and the traveling: "Whatever you do, in word or deed, do everything in the name of the Lord Jesus, giving thanks to God the Father through him" (Colossians 3:17). "Whether you eat or drink, or whatever you do, do all to the glory of God" (1 Corinthians 10:31).

Life has its compartments. Like a house with many rooms in which different activities go on. At home I am a husband. As I pull out of my garage in the morning, I am reminded that I am also a neighbor. When I drive to work, I am a motorist. When I arrive in the office, I am an employee. When I go into a store, I am a customer. When I go to the doctor, I am a patient. When I pay my taxes, I am a citizen. And my calling, as one who has been brought from death to life, is to offer all of these to God.

If you have a boring, tedious job, you can do it in the name of Jesus. If you are caring for a demanding child or an elderly relative, you can offer this as worship to Jesus. And if ill health or some disability changes the course of your life, you can lay this at the feet of Jesus.

Jesus spent three years in public ministry, but before that, He spent two decades working as a carpenter and caring for His mother. And before that, He had a childhood in which He grew in "wisdom and in stature and in favor with God and man" (Luke 2:52). Jesus gave Himself to the Father throughout the entire course of His life, and that means He offered Himself to God as much in His carpentry, in His caring for His mother, and in His childhood as He did when He was preaching the gospel and performing miracles.

I recently hired an electrician to do some work in our house. He did a fine job, and when I got the bill, I noticed that at the top it had the contractors name and at the bottom it said, "A company desiring to bring honor to Jesus Christ through service." I love that! Here was a man who had grasped that he could install lighting for the glory of God.

Take that principle and apply it to every area of your life. If you play soccer, your calling is to offer your soccer to God. That means the way you train, the way you play, the way you encourage a player who is letting the team down, the way you respond to an opponent who fouls you, and even your interactions with the referee will all be pleasing to God. Giving yourself to God means pursuing a pattern of faithfulness and love that honors the Lord in the ordinary routines of life.

When you know who you are and why you are here, you will offer yourself to God. God has brought you from death to life, and the new life He gave you is not to be squandered on living for yourself. Repentance means offering yourself to God and living for Christ, who died and rose for you.

PURSUING THE PATH

Knowing what the path of repentance looks like is one thing; pursuing it is another. We began this book by asking, Why do some people grow in godliness while others seem to make little progress? In this chapter, we will look at three stories of people who failed to find the hidden path. We will see where they got stuck, why they never changed, and, by way of contrast, how our stories can be different.

How would you recognize true repentance in another person? When someone tells you that they are sorry for what they have said or done and that they have changed, how would you know if this is true? How do you know when it is safe to trust? Identifying the distinguishing marks of true repentance will help you to know when you are on the hidden path, and it will help you to discern when someone else has found it.

The Bible speaks of two kinds of sorrow: a worldly kind that leads to death and a godly kind that leads to life: "Godly grief produces a repentance that leads to salvation without regret, whereas worldly grief produces death" (2 Corinthians 7:10).

Being sorry and repenting are clearly different things. You can be sorry without ever changing. You can genuinely regret what you have done without ever repenting. Instead of bringing healing, this worldly grief produces death. It leaves a person bitter and angry, often filled with resentment and sometimes even with despair.

No one wants to live there, and the good news is that there is a better kind of sorrow that produces repentance. This path leads to real and lasting change, and the person who finds it will have no regrets.

What is the difference between the sorrow that destroys and the sorrow that restores? The answer lies in a single word: "godly." "Godly grief produces . . . repentance." The sorrow that restores is God centered, and you will find this godly repentance as you listen to God, draw near to God, and hope in God.

LISTEN TO GOD: CAIN'S STORY

The first distinguishing mark of true repentance is that we listen to God. Imagine yourself in a basement with no light. It's pitch-dark and you struggle to find your way around. The basement is filled with junk that trips you up and sends you sprawling. You don't know where the junk is, so when you go into the basement, you injure yourself repeatedly by falling over the same things time after time.

That's a picture of the human condition. By nature, we are darkened in our understanding (Ephesians 4:18). We don't see the sins that lurk in the dark recesses of our own hearts. While we may be able to see the sins of others, we lack discernment over what needs to change in our own lives. Jesus asked, "Why do you see the speck that is in your brother's eye, but do not notice the log that is in your own eye?" (Matthew 7:3).

The only way we can see the things that cause us to stumble is if God gives us light to see them.

God's Word is like a flashlight that you can take down into the dark places of your own soul. The entrance of God's Word "gives light" (Psalm 119:130), and you will move forward on the path of repentance by listening to God through His Word.

Without the Word, you would continue to stumble around in the dark, like Cain. He never found the hidden path of repentance, because he refused to listen to God. Cain was the first child to be born into the world, and he was the first person to miss the hidden path.

Cain and Abel grew up in a believing family. Their father and mother had seen God with their own eyes. They would have told their sons about how they had walked with God in the Garden of Eden, about how their sin had brought devastating consequences for the entire human family, and about the promise of God that a Savior would triumph over evil and bring hope to the world.

The first family did not have a church to go to, but they

did have an altar—a place of worship where they met with God. One day, Cain and Abel brought offerings, which they presented to God at the altar. Cain, who became the first farmer, brought a sample of his harvest, and Abel, who became the first shepherd, brought a firstborn lamb from his flock.

Scripture tells us that "the Lord had regard for Abel and his offering, but for Cain and his offering he had no regard" (Genesis 4:4–5). How did the first family know this? We're not told, but there is an old tradition that fire came down from heaven and burned up Abel's sacrifice, and I think that may have been the case.

Picture the scene. The first family arrives at the altar. "Boys, this place is special," Adam says. "It's the place where God comes near. Abel you can go first. Place your gift on the altar, offer your prayer, and then stand well back!"

Abel follows his father's instruction. Then, suddenly, to his amazement, fire falls from the sky. It strikes the sacrifice like lightning and burns up the offering. Abel watches wide eyed. God has heard his prayer. God has accepted his sacrifice. The smile of God is upon him.

Then Cain steps up to the altar. With great care, he places his fruit and vegetables on the stones. He offers his prayer, and then steps back, holding his breath in anticipation. But nothing happens. An hour later, Cain's harvest display remains as it was: a gift offered, but evidently not received.

"Cain was very angry, and his face fell." (4:5). *Why did God put on a fireworks display for Abel, and then ignore me? What is so special about Abel and his offering?* The more Cain thought about it, the more humiliated and insulted he felt.

At this point, God spoke to Cain: "Why are you angry, and why has your face fallen? If you do well, will you not be accepted?" (4:6–7). There was a way for Cain to come to God, and the same way is open to all. We come to God not by seeking to impress Him with the work we have done but by trusting in the sacrifice made for us.

Adam and Eve learned the principle of trusting in the sacrifice before they were evicted from the Garden of Eden.

When they sinned, God made "garments of skins and clothed them" (3:21). You can't make a garment of skins without killing an animal, and so it seems that God himself made the first sacrifice and that He did it on the day the first sin was committed. If that were the case, we can be confident that Adam and Eve would have told their boys, "Disobeying God leads to death, but God is gracious, and He will accept the sacrifice of a lamb in our place."

Cain had an open invitation to come to God in the way that God had appointed, but Cain refused to listen. His anger toward God and toward his brother smoldered, and one day when they were out in the fields, Cain killed his brother Abel and became the world's first murderer.

You might think that such a brutal evil would be the end for Cain, but remarkably God spoke to him a second time: "Then the Lord said to Cain, 'Where is Abel your brother?'" (4:9)

God was reaching out to Cain, exposing his sin so that he would have the opportunity to repent. But, again, Cain refused to listen. "Am I my brother's keeper?" he asked.

Four times in this short story we read that God spoke to Cain.

> The Lord said to Cain . . . (4:6)
> Then the Lord said to Cain . . . (4:9)
> And the Lord said . . . (4:10)
> Then the Lord said to him . . . (4:15)

In all likelihood, God spoke to this man in an audible voice, but Cain was not listening.

What Cain said to God tells us a lot about what was going on in his heart. First, he refused to take responsibility for the sin he had committed. When God inquired about Abel, Cain responded: "Am I my brother's keeper?" And second, he was far more concerned about how he would live with the consequences of his sin than he was about the sin itself. "My punishment is greater than I can bear" (4:13).

Cain heard the Word of God, but he refused to listen. He became "a fugitive and a wanderer on the earth" (4:12), running from himself and from his family and living the rest of his life at a distance from God (4:16).

By way of contrast, let's look at a better story. King David sinned greatly. Like Cain, he took another man's life. But David found the hidden path of repentance, and his story has an entirely different outcome.

David's repentance began when God spoke to him through the prophet Nathan, who told him a story about a rich man who had many flocks of sheep and a poor man who only had a single lamb. One day when a traveler came, the rich man took the poor man's lamb to provide a meal for his guest (2 Samuel 12:1–15). Scripture records that "David's anger was greatly kindled against the man" (12:5). He was in the same position as Cain, angry over an apparent injustice. But then the Word of God came to David: "You are the man!" (12:7). And instead of responding with evasion and complaint, as Cain did, David said, "I have sinned against the Lord" (12:13).

Later, in a Psalm expressing his repentance, David said, "Have mercy on me, O God, according to your steadfast love. . . . For I know my transgressions, and my sin is ever before me" (Psalm 51:1–3).

David saw his sin clearly. He faced it without evasion and took responsibility for what he had done. He made no attempt to minimize his offenses. He made no excuses. He made no complaint about the consequences that his sin would bring. David listened to the Word of God, and it brought Him to repentance.

Later, David wrote another Psalm in which he asked God to shine His light into the hidden places of his heart: "Search me, O God, and know my heart! Try me and know my thoughts! And see if there be any grievous way in me, and lead me in the way everlasting!" (Psalm 139:23–24). In other words, David was saying: "Lord, I won't see what's wrong in my life unless you show me, and I won't find the way everlasting unless you lead me. So show me the sin that lurks in my heart. Help me to see what needs to be dealt with! Don't let me drift on without seeing what needs to change in my life. Let your Word be a lamp to my feet and a light to my path" (see Psalm 119:105).

Before we move on, please take a moment to settle what we have learned in your heart. The entrance of God's Word gives light, and you will find the hidden path of repentance as you listen to God through His Word. Without the light of Scripture, you will not be able to see the things that need to change in your life, and you will continue to stumble over the same sins and temptations. So make it your habit to read something from God's Word every day and read with an eye for spotting sins that may be hiding in your soul. For example, when you read that "love is patient" (1 Corinthians 13:4), ask yourself if there are any ways in which you have been impatient. If there are, bring that to God in repentance, place your sin under the blood of Christ, and ask the Lord to help you be more patient going forward. Use the flashlight of the Bible to spot your hidden sins, and you will make progress on the hidden path to a transformed life.

DRAW NEAR TO GOD: ESAU'S STORY

A second example of someone who missed the hidden path is Esau. Like Cain, Esau was the firstborn, and his life was shaped in large measure by conflict with his younger brother.

One day, when Esau came home from hunting, his brother Jacob was cooking stew. Esau was an impulsive man, and being desperate for a meal, he said, "Let me eat some of that red stew, for I am exhausted!" (Genesis 25:30).

Jacob saw an opportunity. Knowing that his brother would be motivated more by impulse than by wisdom, he offered an audacious deal. Jacob would give his brother a bowl of stew if Esau sold his birthright to him (25:31). As the firstborn, Esau would be the head his family and clan in the next generation. This birthright was an honor in any family, but in the family God had chosen to bless, it was an indescribable privilege. Esau would be heir to the promise God had given to Abraham. God's promised blessing would come to the world through his line.

But when Esau came home that day, desperate for a meal, he said, "I am about to die; of what use is a birthright to me?" (25:32). So he sold his birthright for a single meal.

Years later, when Esau's father Isaac was dying, Jacob pulled another stunt, in which he tricked the old man into giving him his brother's blessing. And when Esau discovered that the blessing had been given to Jacob, he burst out with "a loud and bitter cry" (Genesis 27:34 NIV). Esau had what we might call an emotional meltdown. Pain and regret over what he had lost filled his soul, and an agonized scream erupted from the depth of his being.

The book of Hebrews gives us further insight into this story:

> See to it that no one fails to obtain the grace of God; that no "root of bitterness" springs up and causes trouble, and by it many become defiled; that no one is sexually immoral or unholy like Esau, who sold his birthright for a single meal. For you know that afterward, when he desired to inherit the blessing, he was rejected, for he found no chance to repent, though he sought it with tears. (Hebrews 12:15–17)

Esau was filled with regret at his foolish decision to sell his birthright, and his subsequent loss of the firstborn's blessing. He realized that he had been a fool, and he felt his loss so intensely that he yelled out with "a loud and bitter cry." There can be no question about the depth of Esau's regret, but Hebrews tells us that he "found no chance to repent, though he sought it with tears."

Why could Esau not repent? Because, Hebrews tells us, he was "godless": "See that no one is . . . godless like Esau" (12:16 NIV). Esau believed in God, and he wanted the blessing of God so badly that the loss of it brought him to tears. But Esau was godless. In his sorrow, he remained at a distance from God, and that is why he could not repent.

As we saw earlier, Paul distinguishes between "worldly" sorrow that produces death and "godly" sorrow that produces repentance (2 Corinthians 7:10). Repentance involves drawing near to God. It is turning to all that you know of Him, and so a godless person, by definition, cannot repent.

Esau really wanted to change. He "sought" repentance, and he sought it "with tears." But repentance is found not by seeking repentance but by seeking God.

Remaining at a distance from God, Esau missed God's grace and a "root of bitterness" grew up in his soul (Hebrews 12:15). He held a grudge over the wrong that had been done to him, and he consoled himself with the thought of revenge. He felt sorry for himself, he was angry with his brother, and, being godless, he could not find repentance even though he sought it with tears.

When, like Esau, you come to a place of genuine sorrow

over something you have done, you will face an important choice: Will your sorrow drive you farther from God, or will it bring you closer to Him? Esau's story shows that it is possible to feel deep sorrow over something you have done, to have genuine regret, but still to remain at a distance from God. That's worldly sorrow, and nothing good comes from it.

Again, David gives us a better example. He came to God in his sorrow and said, "Create in me a clean heart, O God, and renew a right spirit within me. Cast me not away from your presence, and take not your Holy Spirit from me" (Psalm 51:10–11). David knew that he needed God to walk with him in his sorrow, and in drawing near to God he found true repentance.

Repentance becomes possible when you believe that God will forgive you and that He can change you, but Esau missed the grace of God (Hebrews 12:15).

Commenting on the story of Esau, John Calvin says, "Whenever a sinner sighs on account of his sins, the Lord is ready to pardon him, nor is God's mercy ever sought in vain, for to him who knocks it shall be opened, (Matt 7:8); but . . . the ungodly, however they may deplore their lot, complain and howl, do not yet knock at God's door for mercy, for this cannot be done but by faith."[1]

Pause for a moment to take this in: repentance is an act of faith. David knocked on God's door for mercy because he believed that God would forgive him and that God could change him. Faith makes repentance possible, and you will find the hidden path to a transformed life when you believe that God is ready to forgive you and that He is able to change you.

Faith draws near to God, daring to believe that through Christ He will forgive us and that though the Holy Spirit He can change us. When you see this you will have both the inclination and courage to repent.

HOPE IN GOD: JUDAS' STORY

Like Cain and Esau, Judas Iscariot also missed the hidden path of repentance. After following Jesus for three years, in the inner circle of the twelve disciples, Judas betrayed the

Son of God for a meager thirty pieces of silver.

Scripture tells us that when he saw Jesus was condemned to death, Judas was "seized with remorse and returned the thirty pieces of silver to the chief priests and the elders" (Matthew 27:3 NIV). This may look like repentance, but it was not. Judas' remorse was another example of the "worldly" sorrow that leads to death (2 Corinthians 7:10).

Judas was clearly sorry for what he had done. He knew that he had committed a great sin. He confessed to the priests that he had betrayed innocent blood, and he returned the money he had been paid for his crime (27:4). Why was this not repentance? Because repentance involves hoping in God, and Judas chose despair instead.

The greatest tragedy of Judas' life is not that he betrayed Jesus but that he gave way to despair. If Judas had come to God in repentance, he would have been forgiven. But Judas chose a different path. He gave up on hope, not realizing that Jesus, whom he had betrayed, would rise from the dead and offer forgiveness for the worst of sins.

If you feel close to despair, I want you to know that there is hope for you, but you will not find it by looking back at what you have done. Regret cannot cleanse you. Remorse will not change you. Cain, Esau, and Judas all had bitter regret, but none of them found repentance.

The old hymn, "Rock of Ages," reminds us that we cannot be cleansed by the intensity of our sorrow.

> Could my zeal no respite know,
> Could my tears forever flow,
> All for sin could not atone;
> Thou must save, and Thou alone.[2]

Being sorry will not cleanse you, but Jesus can cleanse you, and He will if you will look to Him in hope.

> Nothing in my hand I bring,
> Simply to Thy cross I cling,
> Naked, come to Thee for dress;
> Helpless, look to Thee for grace;
> Foul, I to the fountain fly:
> Wash me, Savior, or I die!

This is how David prayed to God. He cast himself on God's mercy and dared to hope in Him: "Restore to me the joy of your salvation, and uphold me with a willing spirit" (Psalm 51:12).

DISTINGUISHING MARKS OF TRUE REPENTANCE

In this chapter we have looked at three examples of "worldly," or "godless," sorrow. Cain, Esau, and Judas all had deep regrets and remorse over what they had done, but none of them repented. Cain complained, Esau became bitter, and Judas despaired. Each of them, in his own way, was godless, and none of them found the hidden path of repentance. Instead of listening to God, drawing near to God, and hoping in God, they turned in on themselves and were consumed by regret.

These stories remind us that genuine repentance is not measured by tears: Esau shed tears, but he did not repent. It is not measured by work: Cain built a city, but he did not repent. And it cannot be measured by restitution: Judas returned the money, but he did not repent.

So how can you discern if someone is truly repentant? When trust has been broken this is an intensely practical question: "He says he is sorry, but how do I know if he has really changed? How do I know if her repentance is genuine?"

Repentance is a hidden path, and ultimately a repentant heart is known only to God and to the person who seeks Him. But it does have distinguishing marks, so when you are trying to discern if repentance is genuine, ask this: Is this person listening to God through His Word? Is this person drawing near to God in faith? Is this person looking to God in hope? When you see these things, you have every reason to believe that this person is pursuing the path of repentance and that real and lasting change is taking place in his or her life.

Here is how you can pursue the hidden path to a transformed life: Listen to God through His Word. Build a regular pattern into your life of reading the Bible and use what you read to identify hidden sins. Draw near to God in faith. Ask Him to help you, and trust in Him to change you. Don't give way to despair. There is hope for you in

God's mercy that is yours through Jesus Christ. Practice these things, and you will make progress on the hidden path to a transformed life.

STAYING THE COURSE

Now that you are pursuing the path of repentance, your greatest challenge will be to stay the course. Sooner or later, you will discover that this journey is longer and harder than you had thought. You will face discouragement, and when you do, you may wonder if it is worth pursuing the hidden path and be tempted to give up.

Far from being an occasional event, repentance is a lifelong journey. There will always be more of God for you to discover, more of sin for you to conquer, and more of yourself for you to offer in service to God. So don't expect ever to be satisfied with your repentance. However far you have come in this journey, the long path of repentance stretches out before you. And when you see how far you still have to go, it is easy to get discouraged.

Progress on the path of repentance involves seeing more of your sin, but as you discover hidden sins in your life, you may conclude that your sins are too many and be tempted to give up. As you learn more about yourself, you may decide that your wounds are too deep and that you can no longer be useful to God. And as you discover more about God, you may feel that your faith is too weak and begin to lose hope.

I expect that you already know about these battles. You may wonder, "Why am I not a better man, or a more godly woman? Why is my heart often cold? Why am I not more useful to God? Why have I not made more progress?" If you feel crushed by a sense of your own failure or worn down by the long journey that still lies ahead, this chapter is for you.

HOPE FOR A BROKEN HEART

King David knew what it was like to lament his own failures. Using a vivid analogy, he described his pain as being like broken bones: "Let me hear joy and gladness; let the bones that you have broken rejoice" (Psalm 51:8).

If you have broken an arm or a leg, you know what this is like. You experience great pain, and you need the help of a doctor. When your broken bones are set in a cast, you endure a long period in which your movements are restricted and you may have difficulty in performing simple tasks like walking, washing, or eating.

In using this analogy, David is clear about why his bones were broken. God broke them: "Let the bones *that you have broken* rejoice." The pain David felt as he lamented his sin came as a result of what God was doing in his life. God had convicted David of sin, and David, seeing what was in his heart, felt crushed. But David did not despair. He was convinced that what God had broken, God would heal. And so he prayed that God would cause his broken bones to rejoice.

Then David went further. He brought what was broken and offered it to God:

The sacrifices of God are a broken spirit;
> a broken and contrite heart, O God, you will not
> despise. (51:17)

Having first used the analogy of broken bones to describe what he felt, David tells us what was really broken in his life. His spirit was broken, and a person whose spirit is broken is one who feels that he or she cannot carry on. Then David says that his heart was broken, and a person with a broken heart is one who feels deep pain and sorrow.

What can you do with a broken heart and a broken spirit? David tells us that he brought what was broken to God, daring to believe that God would accept what he offered: "A broken and contrite heart, O God, you will not despise." David offered his broken heart to God because he believed that in God's hands his broken heart would be healed.

No one wants to receive a gift that is broken, so why would God welcome David's broken heart? Because God had done the breaking. And what God breaks, He always heals.

But why would God break David's heart in the first place? Because if God had not exposed David's sin, he would have continued in it and never recovered. God must wound before He can heal.

My grandfather was a gardener, and I remember watching him work with roses when I was growing up. He would take the stem of one plant and the root of another and slice them with a matching cut. Then, he would bind the wounded stem and the wounded root together so that the life of the root would flow into the stem.

The process is known as grafting, and the Bible uses this picture to describe how God gives us new life. James speaks of receiving the "engrafted word" (James 1:21 KJV). The Word of God is sharper than a two-edged sword and sometimes it will wound you (Hebrews 4:12). But as life comes to the wounded stem from the root, God's healing will come to your broken heart because the Holy Spirit has bound you to Christ, who was wounded so that you may be healed.

Suppose for a moment that a gardener, not wanting to wound his plant, simply bound a root and a stem together without making the cut. Being bound together, the stem and the root would look as if they were one, but without the cut, there would be no transfer of life. The life in the root would have no access to the stem, and the stem would die.

Perhaps this is why some people who profess faith show no sign of spiritual life and give no evidence of spiritual growth. A profession of faith without repentance is like binding a stem and a root together without making the cut.

Life flows from the root to the plant through the cut, and a broken heart is a good gift from God because new life can flow through the wound. Knowing your sin and seeing it clearly is painful, like broken bones, but when your heart is broken you can offer it to God, knowing that what He has wounded, He will heal.

God has made life-giving promises to those whose hearts are broken, and these unshakable commitments will help you to stay the course when you are tired of the battle.

God says that He will live with you
For thus says the One who is high and lifted up,
>   who inhabits eternity, whose name is Holy:
"I dwell in the high and holy place,
>   and also with him who is of a contrite and lowly spirit,
to revive the spirit of the lowly,
>   and to revive the heart of the contrite." (Isaiah 57:15)

God lives in two places: He dwells in heaven, described here as "the high and holy place." He also chooses to live with the person who has "a contrite and lowly spirit," and He promises to revive your heart and your spirit by His presence. When you see your own need and feel that you have nothing to offer, God says, "I will move in with you and live with you."

God sent His Son for you

Jesus launched His public ministry in Nazareth, quoting the words of Isaiah about the coming Messiah:

The Spirit of the Lord GOD is upon me,
    because the LORD has anointed me
to bring good news to the poor;
    he has sent me to bind up the brokenhearted.
    (Isaiah 61:1; Luke 4:18)

Jesus came into the world to bind up the broken hearted. The words "bind up" are important because they tell us that Jesus has a ministry of healing toward those whose hearts are broken. He said, "Those who are well have no need of a physician, but those who are sick" (Matthew

9:12). This does not mean that only some people need
Jesus. It means that the people who benefit from the
healing ministry of Jesus are the ones who know that they
are sick and that they cannot heal themselves. When your
heart is broken, you can be confident that Jesus came into
the world for you.

God says that heaven belongs to you

"Blessed are the poor in spirit, for theirs is the kingdom
of heaven" (Matthew 5:3). "Poor in spirit" is another way
of describing a contrite spirit or a broken heart. A person
who is poor in spirit knows that he or she does not have
what God requires and cannot offer what God demands.
But Jesus says that the poor in spirit are blessed. God
lives with them, Christ came for them, and heaven
belongs to them.

It is hard to believe this when your heart is breaking. But
faith takes God at His Word: "You say You will live with the
person who has a contrite spirit—that's me! You say You
sent Your Son to bind up the broken hearted—that's me!
You say heaven belongs to those who know that they cannot
offer what You demand—that's me!"

A broken heart and a contrite spirit are sure evidence of God's grace in your life. God lives with you. Christ came into the world for you. Heaven belongs to you. When God wounds a heart, He will always heal it—so stay the course. And when you see that your sins are many, remember that it is God who opened your eyes. What you see may break your heart, but your ability to see is a gift of grace and a sure sign of hope.

A broken heart is a gift from God; He will not despise it. And if God does not despise a broken heart, neither should you.

STRENGTH FOR A BRUISED REED

Picture yourself walking along a riverbank where tall reeds are blowing in the wind. Some of the reeds are bent over and can barely support their own weight. A strong wind has caught them, thoughtless people have trampled on them, and now these bruised reeds hang limp. Another gust of wind could easily blow them over.

Maybe you can relate to that picture. Strong winds have blown through your life, and other people have pushed you down. You have been bruised, the strength has been taken out of you, and now you are barely holding on. Using this picture, Isaiah says of Jesus that "a bruised reed he will not break" (Isaiah 42:3).

This wonderful promise is vivid for me because in the church I served in London, a group of women met regularly to talk and to sew. They did some beautifully artistic work depicting scenes from the Bible on banners that were displayed on the walls of the church. One of them showed a reed that was bent over and almost broken, but it did not sever because its weight was supported by a hand. The hand could easily have broken the fragile reed, but the way it was positioned beneath the reed made it clear that the hand was there not to break but to support and heal the reed that had been bruised— "A bruised reed he will not break."

As a believer, your bruised life is in the hands of Christ. His strength will hold you up and keep you from breaking. The winds that blow against you and the people who may trample over you are also in His hands.

And God has promised that He will not allow you to be
tested beyond what you can bear. He knows the limits
of your strength, and He has said that He will make a
way for you to carry the load that you bear (1 Corinthians
10:13). You may be bruised, but when you are in the
hands of Christ, you will heal.

There may be times when you feel that your wounds are
so deep that the path to a transformed life is beyond you.
But Christ has a special tenderness towards those who
are bruised, because He knows what it is to be bruised
Himself. He knows what it is like to be abandoned,
wounded, and horribly abused. And when your wounds are
deep, He will hold you, support you, and lovingly heal you.

FUEL FOR A SMOLDERING FLAME

Picture yourself trying to start a fire using only a few leaves
and twigs. The leaves are damp, and it's hard to get the
fire going. At first it seems that there's more smoke than
fire, and as you look at the smoking twigs, you may wonder
if there's any fire there at all. Isaiah takes up that picture

and says of Jesus that "a faintly burning wick he will not quench" (Isaiah 42:3).

There will be times in your journey when you feel discouraged by your lack of progress on the hidden path. You may wonder, "Does God really want someone whose faith is as weak as mine? Can He have any use for someone as messed up as me?"

The flame of your faith may be obscured by the smoke of your own folly, and when you see more smoke than fire, you may wonder if there is any fire at all. But smoke and fire are found together. The old saying is true: "There's no smoke without fire." And the Bible gives us many examples of how the fire of faith and the smoke of folly are found in the same person at the same time.[1]

When Peter confessed his faith in Jesus, he said, "You are the Christ" (Matthew 16:16). That was the fire of faith. Jesus said, "Flesh and blood has not revealed this to you, but my Father who is in heaven" (16:17). But moments later, Peter rebuked Jesus, who had just announced that He was going to Jerusalem where He would suffer and die.

"Far be it from you, Lord," Peter said, "this shall never happen to you" (16:22). Mixed with the fire of Peter's faith was the smoke of his folly.

When Thomas said, "Unless I see in his hands the mark of the nails . . . and place my hand into his side, I will never believe" (John 20:25), that was smoke. When he confessed Jesus as "my Lord and my God" (20:28), that was fire.

When our Lord told a distraught father that "all things are possible for one who believes" (Mark 9:23), the man said, "I believe" (9:24). That's fire! But in the next breath, he said, "Help my unbelief!" (9:24). That's smoke.

In the Garden of Gethsemane, Jesus told His disciples to watch and pray. "The spirit indeed is willing," He said. That's fire. "But the flesh is weak" (Matthew 26:41). That's smoke.

Paul said, "O wretched man that I am! Who will deliver me from this body of death?" (Romans 7:24). That's smoke. But then he says, "Thanks be to God through Jesus Christ our Lord!" (Romans 7:25). That's fire.

The fire of faith and the smoke of folly are always found together in the life of a Christian believer. The proportions will vary, but there is no smoke without fire, and there is no fire without smoke.

Writing in the seventeenth century, Richard Sibbes says, "Grace does not do away with corruption all at once. But some is left for believers to fight with." For this reason, he points out, Christians will see themselves in a different light depending on whether they are focused more on what Christ has done in their lives or more on what still remains to be done.[2]

So where should we look? Sibbes wisely counsels that "we must have two eyes, one to see imperfections in ourselves . . . the other to see what is good." A clear view of our own sins will keep us on the path of repentance, and a clear view of the grace that is ours in Christ will keep us moving forward. The fire and the smoke both contribute to our journey on the path of repentance. We need one eye to see the fire and one eye to see the smoke. And when we see both, we will make progress.

Your faith may be like a flickering flame, but even weak faith is a gift from God. So don't make the mistake of thinking that you do not have faith at all because the fire of faith does not burn as brightly in you as it does in others.[3]

When Peter writes his second letter, he addresses it to "those who have obtained a faith of *equal standing* with ours" (2 Peter 1:1, italics added). He does not say that all Christians have a faith of equal *strength*, but he describes all Christian as having a faith of equal *standing* with the faith of the apostles.

The believer with the weakest faith belongs to Christ as surely as the one whose faith is strong. When you believe in the Lord Jesus Christ, you are trusting in the same Savior as the apostle Peter and the apostle Paul. Your faith may not be as strong as theirs, but the smallest spark of faith is as much a gift of God as the roaring flame.

The Holy Spirit kindles the fire of faith in smoky souls. You can be confident that when God starts a fire, He will never snuff it out. When your faith burns low, the Holy Spirit will blow on the embers and kindle a flame. Sibbes says, "See a flame in a spark, a tree in a seed. See great things in little beginnings. Look not so much to the beginning as to the perfection, and so we shall be, in some degree, joyful in ourselves, and thankful to Christ."[4]

When you look at your Christian life, you will often feel that you are not what you *ought* to be and that you are not what you *want* to be. Remember too that you are not what you *used* to be, and press on to what, by God's grace, you will become.

SURPRISED BY JOY

Repentance is a journey in which we continue to learn more about sin, more about ourselves, and more about God, and it is a joyful journey because it leads to a transformed life.

Repentance and *joy* may not seem like words that go together, but Jesus said that there is joy in heaven over one sinner who repents (Luke 15:7, 10). And if there is joy over repentance in heaven, there will be joy in repentance for you.

Sin always makes a believer miserable. It offers just enough pleasure to tempt us, but the promise is empty, and it soon gives way to regret. True happiness is found not in pursuing sin but in getting free from it. The pursuit of repentance is a pursuit of joy.

C. S. Lewis described three kinds of people, the first being "those who live simply for their own sake and pleasure, regarding Man and Nature as so much raw material to be cut up into whatever shape may serve them."[1]

Jesus told a story about a man who lived for himself (Luke 12:16–20). His fields produced a good crop, and, when he saw that his harvest would exceed his storage capacity, he decided to pull down his barns and rebuild on a larger scale. He looked forward to the day when he would be able to say to himself, "you have ample goods laid up for many years; relax, eat, drink, be merry" (12:19). But while this man was still making his plans, he died. And God called him a fool (12:20).

The folly of this man was not that he wanted to build bigger barns, but that he lived for himself and was "not rich toward God" (12:21). With all of his resources, this man could have done a great deal to help others, but his focus was entirely on himself and his own comfort:

> *I* will tear down *my* barns and build larger ones, and there *I* will store all *my* grain and *my* goods. And *I* will

say to *my* soul, "Soul . . . relax, eat, drink, be merry."
(Luke 12:18–19)

To become consumed with yourself—your rights, your
dreams, your plans, your achievements, your comforts, and
your security—is to live like a fool. No one in their right
mind wants to go there.

THE MISERY OF MERE DUTY

Lewis then describes a second type of person:

> In the second class are those who acknowledge some other claim
> upon them—the will of God, the categorical imperative, or the
> good of society—and honestly try to pursue their own interests
> no further than this claim will allow. They try to surrender to the
> higher claim as much as it demands, like men paying a tax, but
> hope, like other taxpayers, that what is left over will be enough
> for them to live on. Their life is divided, like a soldier's or a
> schoolboy's life, into time "on parade" and "off parade," "in
> school" and "out of school."[2]

Later, Lewis adds this striking observation:

> The members of the second class (to which most of us belong)

are always and necessarily unhappy. The tax which moral conscience levies on our desires does not in fact leave us enough to live on. As long as we are in this class we must either feel guilt because we have not paid the tax or penury because we have.[3]

The Gospels record the story of the rich young ruler, a moral and upright man who asked Jesus, "What must I do to inherit eternal life?" (Luke 18:18). Jesus quoted the Ten Commandments: "Do not commit adultery, Do not murder, Do not steal, Do not bear false witness, Honor your father and mother" (18:20). The man replied, "All these I have kept from my youth" (18:21). He felt sure that he had kept the commandments. Was there anything else that he needed to do?

Jesus said, "One thing you still lack. Sell all that you have and distribute to the poor, and you will have treasure in heaven; and come, follow me" (18:22). The man had pursued a life of duty, but Jesus was calling him to a life of love. If this man truly loved God with all his heart, and if he truly loved his neighbors as much as he loved himself, he would have been glad to give all that he had to the poor and to come and follow Jesus. But this man felt that Jesus was asking too much. His face fell and he went away sorrowful (Mark 10:22).

If you obey God only out of a sense of duty, you will often feel that God is asking too much. Lewis says most of us are in this second class, and as long as we remain in this position, we can never be happy. Giving will feel like paying taxes. Following Jesus will seem like the right thing to do, but you will find no pleasure in doing it.

If our only choices were to live the life of a fool or to live a life of duty, we would always be unhappy. But thank God, there is another way.

THE JOY OF A CHANGED HEART

After describing the person who lives for him- or herself and the one who pursues a moral life out of a sense of duty, C. S. Lewis describes a third kind of person whose life is marked by joy:

> The third class is of those who can say like St Paul that for them "to live is Christ." These people have got rid of the tiresome business of adjusting the rival claims of Self and God by the simple expedient of

rejecting the claims of Self altogether. The old egoistic will has been turned round, reconditioned, and made into a new thing. The will of Christ no longer limits theirs; it *is* theirs. All their time, in belonging to Him, belongs also to them, for they are His.[4]

The Gospels record the story of a man called Zacchaeus who had risen to the position of being a chief tax collector, a profession that was notorious for corruption and extortion. When Jesus passed through Jericho, He called out to Zacchaeus, who was hiding in a tree: "Zacchaeus, hurry and come down, for I must stay at your house today" (Luke 19:5). We are not told about the conversation with Zacchaeus in his house, but we know what happened as a result. Zacchaeus said, "Behold, Lord, the half of my goods I give to the poor. And if I have defrauded anyone of anything, I restore it fourfold" (19:8).

The most striking thing here is that Zacchaeus offered to do something Jesus didn't even ask! This came from his heart. It was something that he *wanted* to do. Put Zacchaeus alongside the rich young ruler and you will see how different they are. The ruler asked what he *must* do: "What must I do to inherit eternal life?" (18:18). Zacchaeus found joy in what he *could* do: "Lord, the half of my goods I give to the poor" (19:8).

Like the rich fool and the rich young ruler, Zacchaeus had been all about himself. He had made his money by cheating and stealing. But his response to Jesus was marked by freedom and joy.

Jesus said to Zacchaeus, "Today, salvation has come to this house" (19:9). Salvation involves a change of heart in which a person pursues a life of love with freedom and joy. Dane Ortlund says it well: "Conversion is . . . the divine granting of a new love for God such that holiness appears beautiful instead of ugly, while sin becomes repulsive instead of attractive."[5]

Repentance is more than duty, more than morality, and more than something you must do to have eternal life. It is the hidden path to a transformed life, and as you pursue it, you will be surprised by joy.

THE LONG JOURNEY HOME

We have seen that repentance, the hidden path to a transformed life, involves turning from as much as you know of your sin to give as much as you know of yourself to as much as you know of your God.

God's grace makes repentance possible. The inclination to repent comes when the Holy Spirit shows you the extent of your own sin, and the courage to repent comes when the Holy Spirit shows you the extent of Christ's love.

Perhaps the best known of Jesus' stories is the parable of the prodigal son, who said, "Father, give me the share of property that is coming to me" (Luke 15:12). Then the son went into a distant country and wasted everything he had on riotous living (15:13–16). After some time, there was a famine in that country, and, running out of options, the prodigal decided to return to his father.

The three elements of repentance that we've explored in this book are all present in the story of the prodigal son.

Turning from All That You Know of Your Sin

The prodigal son came to his senses and realized the futility of his rebellion. He said, "I will arise and go to my father, and I will say to him, 'Father, I have *sinned* against heaven and before you'" (15:18, italics added).

Turning to All That You Know of God

The prodigal son believed that returning home would be better than remaining in the far country: "My father's hired servants have more than enough bread, but I perish here with hunger!" (15:17). He believed that his father would receive him, and this gave him hope as he began the long journey home.

Giving All That You Know of Yourself

The prodigal son offered himself in the service of his father. Although he no longer saw himself as a dearly loved son, he decided to say to his father: "Treat me as one of your hired servants" (15:19).

The long journey home could not have been easy for the prodigal son. Dark clouds of guilt and shame filled his horizon as he took his first steps on the path of repentance.

He had rehearsed his speech: "I will say to him, "Father, I have sinned against heaven and before you" (15:18).

The son began his journey of repentance out of necessity. He had no food, and his money was gone. It was time to humble himself, own what he had done, and return home. It was his duty. It was the right thing to do.

But while the son was still a long way off, his father ran out to meet him (15:20). Filled with joy, the father embraced his son and kissed him. "Bring quickly the best robe, and put it on him," he said, "and put a ring on his hand, and shoes on his feet. . . . Let us eat and celebrate. For this my son was dead, and is alive again; he was lost, and is found" (15:22–24).

The father in Jesus' story was far more generous than the son would ever have dared to imagine. Instead of being consumed by a sense of guilt, the son was caught up in his father's joy. And instead of enduring a life sentence of shame, the son wore a robe and a ring, given by his father. After wasting so much in the far country, the prodigal son had nothing to celebrate in himself, but he found joy in the grace, mercy, patience, and kindness of the father, whose love had never let him go.

Jesus wants you to know that this is how God the Father will receive you when you come to Him in repentance. He will clothe you in Christ's righteousness, He will place the ring on your finger, signifying that you are His son or daughter, and, as He welcomes you home, you will share in His joy.

ENDNOTES

Introduction

[1] John Calvin, *The Institutes of the Christian Religion*, 3.3.2.

[2] J. I. Packer, *Keep in Step with the Spirit: Finding Fullness in Our Walk with God*, 2nd ed. (Grand Rapids, MI: Baker Books, 2005), 87.

1. Knowing God

[1] Mike Mason, *The Gospel According to Job* (Wheaton, IL: Crossway, 1994) 428.

[2] Packer, *Keep in Step,* 87. Italics added.

2. Leaving Sin

[1] Sinclair B. Ferguson, *The Christian Life: A Doctrinal Introduction* (Edinburgh: Banner of Truth, 1989), 156.

[2] John Owen, *The Mortification of Sin* (Edinburgh: Banner of Truth, 2004), 37. Italics added

[3] Owen, *Mortification of Sin,* 86.

[4] Owen, *Mortification of Sin,* 8.

[5] Owen, *Mortification of Sin*, 5.

[6] Cited in John Stott, *Only One Way: The Message of Galatians* (Downers Grove, IL: InterVarsity Press, 1968), 151.

[7] Ferguson, *Christian Life,* 162.

[8] Owen, *Mortification of Sin,* 5.

[9] Owen, *Mortification of Sin*, 117.

4. Pursuing the Path

[1] John Calvin, *Commentaries on the Epistle of Paul the Apostle to the Hebrews* (Edinburgh: 1853), 329.

[2] Augustus Toplady, *Rock of Ages* (1775).

5. Staying the Course

[1] I have adapted the following examples from Richard Sibbes, *The Bruised Reed* (1630; repr., Edinburgh: Banner of Truth, 1998), 18-19.

[2] Sibbes, *Bruised Reed*, 35.

[3] Sibbes, *Bruised Reed*, 124.

6 Surprised by Joy

[1] C. S. Lewis, *Present Concerns* (London: Collins, 1986), 21, quoted in Dane Ortlund, *A New Inner Relish* (Fearn, UK: Christian Focus, 2008).

[2] Lewis, *Present Concerns,* 21.

[3] Lewis, *Present Concerns,* 21–22.

[4] Lewis, *Present Concerns*, 21.

[5] Ortlund, *New Inner Relish,* 173.

ACKNOWLEDGMENTS

I would like to express my heartfelt thanks to all who have contributed to this book.

First among them is Davis Wetherell, whose skillful hand was on the beginning and the end of this project. Davis prepared a first draft of the opening chapters from a series of sermons I preached some years ago, and then proofed and polished the final manuscript when it was done. Davis, who now works at Crossway as a Bible proofreader and copyeditor, served on our team at Unlocking the Bible. We still miss you Davis, but we are thankful for the ministry God has trusted to you.

Gina O'Brien, who serves as Director of Ministry Resources with Unlocking the Bible, has overseen the production of this book. Her team includes Shannon Hannasch, who designed the layout and the cover. Gina, you were the first to believe that the repentance series should be reworked as a book. You suggested this some years ago, and I am so glad that you did.

It has again been my joy to work with my friend and colleague, Tim Augustyn, on this project. Tim's wisdom as a pastor and skill as a writer are a great gift to me and to all who serve with Unlocking the Bible. When we meet to review what I have written, Tim's wise counsel, his gift with words, and his eye for detail make what we have at the end better by far than what I brought at the beginning. Thank you, Tim for your tireless commitment to this work.

I am also grateful to my son Andrew, and my wife, Karen, who read these chapters as I was working on them and made helpful suggestions. Karen, your patience and constant encouragement are a special gift for which I am truly thankful.

Finally, I would like to thank the many people whose faces have been in my mind as I have worked on these pages. One of my privileges as a pastor is to speak with people who are seeking help and counsel as they walk the path of repentance. The places where I surmise what readers may think or feel arise either from my own experience or from the experience of others who have told me about their struggles. May the Lord use this book to encourage you, and all who read it, to keep moving forward on the hidden path to a transformed life.

Colin S. Smith
Thanksgiving, 2020

UNLOCKING
THE
B|BLE

Published by Unlocking the Bible
PO Box 3454, Barrington, IL 60011
Email: info@unlockingthebible.org
Website: www.unlockingthebible.org

Printed in the United States of America